T0381453

Poetry:
Faith Filled Testimony

THOMAS BETTY

WestBow Press books may be ordered through booksellers or by contacting:

WestBow Press
A Division of Thomas Nelson & Zondervan
1663 Liberty Drive
Bloomington, IN 47403
www.westbowpress.com
844-714-3454

ISBN: 979-8-3850-3064-4 (sc)
ISBN: 979-8-3850-3065-1 (e)

Library of Congress Control Number: 2024916216

Print information available on the last page.

WestBow Press rev. date: 08/13/2024

Contents

Life

Life is complicated
no one knows why

Someone deciding to join the army
getting sent overseas
causing their family to have depression

It's just life though
everyone has to deal with it

I feel like I got the worst
always depressed
always thinking
can't figure anything out

Why am I still single
why did nothing go the way I saw it
I just can't quite figure myself out

People think life is easy
think again

Put yourself in my shoes
and see how it is for me

You would be begging to get out
you would just want to die

Life isn't easy for anyone
everyone has their doubts

At some point in life
and if you never did

Then you have a perfect life
which no one can have

There is no such thing as one
even if you think you have one
sin has caused devastation

If you think once about something
then start doubting it
you do not have a good life
or a perfect life

You start to feel miserable
and just want out

A Sin From the Deep

It is red, fire, and deep
It makes innocent weep
It is a sin from hell
The innocent always dwell
The devil gets his way
The sinners kill if they may
It takes the innocent and/or money
It leaves a trail of red and bloody
The sinner, who does it, does it for a need
But in the right eye it is not a deed
It may sentence them too life
So it may take strife
This makes it pleased in a way
But it happens every day

Bullying

The child sits there
taking the pill
he stole from his mom

She doesn't know this
doesn't know what's been happening

Going up to a stranger
giving the man money

Buying a drug
that can take his life
in seconds

Depression building up
he's ready to explode
the lab just did down the road

He hears the sirens
thinking they are coming for him

The bullying keeps happening
making the cuts deeper

There is enough blood
to save someone's life

He doesn't care about anyone
he takes his dad's gun

Puts it to his head
wondering if this is the end

Questioning if anyone will miss him
they find him dead

People saw that he was bullied
but it was too late

Reality

What is real
And not
We try to figure it out
We question everything in life
Where did we come from
Who are we
Did a superior being make us in His image
Or does Anthropology tell the truth
That humans came from apes
Are there myths
That are real
But haven't seen
Or figured out
Does another human life form exist
Is there more than one God
That makes the world go round
And causes bad things to happen
Is the world going to end
Why do people keep saying it
Why do they show it getting destroyed
People still predicting
Searching for the answers
I'm one of them
Wanting to know the truth
About everything
Wanting to know
Reality

Suicidal Thoughts

Suicidal thoughts running through my head
Wondering why I'm not dead
Everyone asks and wonders why
They say why can't you just pray
They don't realize
Even though it may be a choice
Once the thoughts of hopelessness
And the fear of being alone hits
It causes the depression
The hurt and anxiety
To sit in so deep
We cry out in need
Looking and searching for that one person
To drop what they are doing
To come and just be by our side

Depression

Depression setting in
wondering why this is happening

Trying to show that we are strong
praying and hoping it doesn't last long

Sitting at home
feeling all alone

Even though we have our loved ones
we are supposed to be the leaders

Deep down we are lost
trying to figure out at what cost

What are we supposed to do
besides sit in our room

Grab your loved ones
take your families

Do a Bible study
just don't go nutty

Blast some music
praise and worship

Knowing God is in control
He will make us feel whole

The battle has already been won
by the death of His Son

Don't gloom in fret
we know He paid our debt

The end of this is in sight
the end of the tunnel is bright

Once we come together again
we get to sing, worship, and praise Him
knowing He had a plan

Dear Younger Tom

Young Tom
There are many days you will feel numb
Days where you will feel lonely
Feel like there is no one
I know there have been many questions
Bringing you in many directions
Around and around in your head
Wishing you were dead
I am here to tell you
I will do my best to help you through
All the doubts and worries
As I am still dealing with all the hurts
One day you will wake up
Realize all those dreams you made up
Thinking a relationship is what defines you
Only to realize it's only going to hurt you
Send you down a road
That will only make you feel more lonely and cold
But I am here to say
There is always a way
A way out of the darkness
To be free from the harness
You have to let go
I know it is easy to say no
But in the end
You have to give up your hand

Let Him take the wheel
Because this is the only way you will heal
You will find who you are
You will become a bright shining star
Not the type of star you always wanted to be
But open up your eyes so you can see
You are a light in this world
Even if you think you were unheard
You will make a difference
Even if that is helping one person be of deliverance
I know you have the fear
Wondering if the end is near
Asking what happens if you die
Wondering if life was a lie
Pick up your head
Get off your bed
Follow me
We will go see
Together my friend
That there is no end

Changing the World

A hero may be fast
But they don't last
A hero may be strong
But they don't live long
They are just symbols
That portray the real hero's
The one's that live in the Spirit
Not in the flesh
They are themselves
Always in the crowds
Always in the dark
Living in the night
But they are a shining light
Showing the way
They are the one's
That always pray
They are God's warriors
God's hero's
Always changing the World

Realize

When you realize
All that He has done
You wonder
What else He can do
All the love
All the compassion
All the sin
The doubt
Anger and sadness
He put on Himself
Only to sacrifice it all
For you and me
His life taken
So our eyes are open
Open your heart
Your soul
Let the spirit
Fill it all
Let that empty hole
Be filled with love
Give your life to Him
Take the journey of faith
To restoration
And sanctification

Real Eyes

One day you will realize
You will see through real eyes
Mistakes you will regret
Faults you wish you could take back
Decisions you wish you could have changed
And done differently
When that day comes
You can think to the past
Think of high school
Being a football player
Or joining the drama class
But don't dwell
Realize it could not last
You may wish your life could be better
You could be in a different place
But Search
Seek out for Him
And you will see
You are in the place
You are supposed to be

Second Chances

There is such a thing
As second chances
Second chances
To live, laugh, and love
Second chances
To never look back
To keep moving forward
When a door closes
Another one will open
Second chances
To be born again
In the body, soul
But mainly the Spirit
The chance
To know God
And Jesus Christ
For who they are
Through the Holy Spirit

Yolo

People say
You only live once
But I can prove
That isn't true
I got the chance
The chance of a life time
The second chance
Everyone asks for
To live a second life
I had the gun
To my head
Could have pulled the trigger
Should have been dead
But couldn't load it
Could feel it wasn't the end
There is more to this
More to this life
People can't see
But I got to see
What this life can offer
We are all a gift
A gift from God
Who is God?

The one who gave me a second chance
How do you know?
He was with me that night
I could feel His presence
Could see the Holy Spirit
Jesus Himself
Telling me there's more
To put the gun away

Load and Pull

Yolo
You only live once
Says who?
Only you
Can make that decision
Decision to load
And pull
Decision to believe
Decision to have faith
Faith in God
The one true God
That gave me a second chance
The chance to live
And be free
In my will
But His as well
The chance to be telling you
It's your decision
To believe
So decide
Do you load
Pull?
And say Yolo?

End in Sight

We sit here in darkness
not knowing what the end game is

Many of us stay home
emotionally and spiritually feeling alone

Questioning what the outcome may be
feeling that there is something we need

We are used of being here and there
running around and going everywhere

Now we sit at home bored
trying to figure out how to fill that void

Trying to remember our hobbies
binge watching our favorite movies

Thinking all we can do is Netflix and chill
we should be thinking and asking what is His will

Doing what we can to glorify Him
not letting our Faith go dim

Stopping and taking that step back
to see what we lack

Seeing what we have been missing
realize we have been losing

Sight of who we are
the reality of every single scar

That we have forced ourselves to forget
don't sit in fear and sweat

Take a breath and focus on Him
truly ask and repent all your sins

See what you have been missing
what this world has been missing

True faith and belief in Him
pray and see He will win

We need to be His light
there is an end in sight

Faith

Faith doesn't come in a day
Faith doesn't come in a night
You have to ask and pray
In order to have the might
Be patient and wait
His timing is right
He will make your path straight
And help you win the fight
But watch what you do
The devil lurks within
He is waiting for you
To fall into sin
Your faith will be strong
He will be weak
It won't be long
Until you are on top of the peak

Gifts

Everything you do
Everything you are good at
Say because it's just you
It's called just a talent
But that isn't true
It's not just a talent
God calls them a Gift
He gave them to us
So we can lift
And bring others up
He uses them
To bring light and glory
Into His kingdom
So everyone can be saved and holy
These gifts
Makes a person
Without these gifts
There is no reason
For humans to exist

Stop and Believe

If you put God first
You will never die of thirst
Rely on Him
Life will never be dim
Be full of everlasting light
God always wins the fight
You've asked Him why
Believed it's a lie
Stop and Believe
Have faith
And you shall see
It's all true
He is there for you
Ask and you shall receive
Have patience though
It's not your time
But His time
He is always right
Look further into life
Strive to seek Him
And you shall see the light

His Living Water

We get thirsty
We search for a well
When it's empty
We can tell
Something is missing
There is a hole
We feel nothing
We ask where's our soul
Jesus come knocking
We pray for our life
What He tells us, is shocking
To have eternal life
All we need to do
Is drink His water
If this we knew
We wouldn't need water

The Anchor of Hope

There was a time
When humans thought they knew all
That they were higher than the great Divine
This was the time of their fall
We try to sail our own ships
Do our best to stay afloat
But once we start sinking
We rely on ourselves to refloat
We try to patch the holes
Mend the broken pieces
Think we are in control
Try to figure out the reasons
Even though we screwed up
Causing damage by being a canker
We don't like to stop
To call and rely on our anchor
What we don't realize
Is we need something to keep us up
We want someone to hear our cries
Why don't we just wakeup
Open our eyes
To see the one and only light
Giving us a hand to rise

Don't let the anchor be an afterthought
When the ship starts to sink
The anchor should be first
Make it an instinct
There are other things that are worse
Call and rely on this anchor of hope
For sinkable ships
Will become unsinkable

The King and the Sacrifice

The King of the jungle
But yet so humble
The helplessness of the fields
But the only one who heals
He gives out punishment
But with fair judgement
He may have submitted
But was not defeated
He may have all the power
But was still devoured
He is full of peace
But was considered a disgrace
He is the King of kings
But had to deal with suffering
The sacrifice for our sins
But this is the only way He could win

Encounter

The Holy Spirit flows
Everything starts to glow
Mind starts pacing
Heart starts racing
Palms get sweaty
Eyes get teary
Hands start raising
Breath gets taken
Look up into the sky
Realize why
Encounter

I've Been Thinking of You

Time after time
You ask the questions when and why
Day after day
You look and ask for a way
When you don't see or hear
You question if He is even there
You feel alone and lost
Wandering away at your own cost
Becoming one of the ninety-nine
Believing and telling yourself you are fine
You feel a tug
Telling you to look up
You see a hand
You hear take my hand
Realizing it's the one and only
You no longer feel lonely
You look around
Noticing footprints on the ground
Realizing they aren't yours
But the saviors
He's been there
Carrying you everywhere
He's never left your side
Even though you keep trying to hide
You think He forgets about you
But He always thinks of you

God's Love

Some people see nails
The last nail in the coffin
The end of a tale
Everything will be forgotten
With nails in His hand
Blood on the cross
Everything pointed to the end
Everyone started to feel the loss
He was presumed dead
They didn't see God's plan
Even though they were led
They were scared and ran
When everything was dark
Everything seemed dead
Flowers and vines became the mark
Where He laid on that bed
The sign of life
Darkness taken over by the light
So, don't take strife
Sing and rejoice in delight
He gave us His Son
So, we can fly with Him above
The war is won
So, we can feel God's love

There's No One Like You

Let there be light
Let you shine bright
There's no one like you
Let us be made new
Only in your image
Let us not be damaged
Sin will not destroy us
Your grace will only grow us
Death does not exist
Help us resist
God is graceful
He is peaceful
We only love you
We know you are true
Restoration is present
We repent
Our heart is yours
There's no such thing as lows
Everything is up from here
Mountains can't hold us back anymore

Shattered and Torn

Shattered and torn
Always feeling worn
Questions running through my head
Where am I being led
Keeps feeling like I am running
Always find myself doubting
Feeling you are the one
Is where the journey had begun
Everything points to you
Keep asking Him if it's true
He keeps telling me to wait
That's one thing that I hate
Not knowing how long
I sit here, listening to a song
Making me think of you
Seeing the time, I fell in love with you
Pieces of my broken heart
Is where it had to start
I know I have God
I feel He gave me the nod

I Know I have God

I feel He gave me the nod
I know I have God
Is where it had to start
Pieces of my broken heart
Seeing the time, I fell in love with you
Making me think of you
I sit here, listening to a song
Not knowing how long
That's one thing that I hate
He keeps telling me to wait
Keep asking Him if it's true
Everything points to you
Is where the journey had begun
Feeling you are the one
Always find myself doubting
Keeps feeling like I am running
Where am I being led
Questions running through my head
Always feeling worn
Shattered and torn

God is There for You

You may think
you have gotten good at holding it in
that's not what I think

You may feel broken
you may feel hurt

May say the tears are from hurting
I say they are tears of healing

God is a healer
He brings up the brokenness
so we can heal from the past

Each tear we cry
they are tears of freedom
tears of healing

Just like the song
there is freedom in every drop
sometimes the only way to heal a broken heart
is when we fall apart

If you weren't healing
you wouldn't be willing
to ask for help

That's why I can't walk away
that's why I won't give up
that's why I say I truly forgive you

You won't give up on me
you keep forgiving me
even though you could have walked away

You are not broken
but Gods woken child

Shining as a bright light
in this broken dark world

Showing the rest of the broken people
there is a God that loves them
and is willing to heal them

I'm here Till the End

I know you are hurting
I know you are in pain
I may not know how you feel
But I know you understand
I'm happy and grateful
You are trying
I will never quit
I will never give up on you
If you never give up on me
With God everything will get better
This happened before
No matter what you go through
I will always be there
I believe and have faith you can get
through anything
No matter how rough it gets
He still loves you
It will get better soon again just like the last
time
You can get through this
I'm here till the end

H.O.P.E

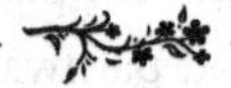

H stands for home
A place many can come
Call their own
And not feel alone
Everyone is welcomed
Even though you may not be a friend
You will be a part of the family
Now that is reality
No matter what you may have done
He still sent His only Son
To show us
That He not only loves us
But that we are His children

O stands for orphan
Or orphans
What everyone is
Before He lets us in
We were all homeless
Always feeling hopeless
Bound in chains
Always dealing with pains
Always feeling low
With no where to go
The only way to be freed
Is by being loved

P stands for passage
And pathway
The way to a better life
Free of all the strife
An open door
A way out from always being torn
To follow the light
That burns bright
Away from all the dark
To where He left His mark
For all to be free
And to see
Who He truly is

E stands for enlighten
Not only to be lightened
Shown to open the door
To know Him more
But to know who you are
You do not have to go far
Just stand in front and look into the mirror
You will see clearer
That not only will you see yourself
But He too will see Himself
We are made in the image of God
And no one can take that away from us